Bricks & Bones

The Endearing Legacy and Nitty Gritty Phenomenon of The Indy 500

Tony Borroz

Copyright (C) 2017 - Anthony Borroz
Bricks & Bones
The Endearing Legacy and Nitty-Gritty Phenomenon of The Indy 500
By Tony Borroz
Edited by Dora Badger - Woodward Press
Edition 1.0 - Jun 2017
Published by Automoblog.net under Gearhead Media, LLC

Images: Dreamstime.com, St Elmo Steakhouse (p 12, 13, 15), Carl Anthony (p 45)

CONTENTS

Prologue: The Indy 500 is Pure Righteousness

Conflicting Emotions

I'm sitting in Dallas/Fort Worth International Airport, between here and there, between desert and farmland, between my glowering past and my immediate future. I am calm, but my mind seems to be screaming out in a thousand different directions at once. Everyone tells me I should be feeling happy or excited or sad or tired or respectful or lonely, but I'm all those things and none of them at the same time.

At the moment, I am still. Waiting through this interminable layover, waiting for my connecting flight between here and there.

Frequent Fear

My mind, and a notional team of psychiatrists would imply that, in my given emotional state outside of "work" (which this is), peace and serenity would be good goals to pursue. Instead, I am anxious to stuff myself into an alloy tube controlled by overworked, overtired, and overpaid former-military hotshots; and staffed by over-glorified waitstaff who, these days, seem to have no compunction about physically and emotionally abusing you for the slightest infractions like airborne Stassi martinets.

Powerful Prelude

I should be still... be still... be still and seek out an extended period of immobility, but right now what I am most anxious for is speed, and lots of it. I need to wad myself into an alloy tube and be blasting through the thin air at .84 Mach. I need velocity and quickness, pace, and swiftness.

I am going to The Indy 500.

Chapter 1: Real Wrong

Due to scheduling issues, I am unable to make it to Speedway, Indiana for qualifying for the 500. Qualifying for this race is, in a lot of ways, overly complex and more convoluted than it needs to be. It also makes for one of the hardest things a race car driver can do. Unlike other series, or other races for that matter, that require you to qualify by doing one lap, making it into the field of The Indy 500 obliges you to do four contiguous laps.

All four laps are back to back, and the average speed over those four laps determines where you start on Memorial Day. Mess up one lap– shoot, mess up one *corner* – and the rest of your qualifying run is ruined. Drivers universally say it is the most nerve wracking thing they are asked to do. Lots of the crazy-brave can hang it out over the edge for a single lap, grit their teeth and hand over trust to luck or skill or bravery and be okay.

Having to roll the dice four times when your life is on the line, well, that's a different calculation.

Go Green

So, as usual, here I sit on a rather fine Sunday spring morning, watching race cars on TV. Qualifying is run in reverse order, with each succeeding car having practiced faster than the one before it. As we get into the really fast guys, up comes Sebastien Bourdais. French, tall, with brownish hair, blue eyes, and a tendency to be quietly humorous, Bourdais is a four-time CART champion, a feat he pulled off by winning all four of his championships in a row. No one had done that before him, and no one will ever beat it now that CART has merged with the Indy Racing League. He is, in short, not a guy to be trifled with.

Bourdais takes the green and right from the start, he is on it! I mean the accelerator might as well be welded to the bulkhead.

Lap 1: 231 mph and change.

Lap 2: 231 mph and change, but a fraction faster.

He is cranking them off. Until now, the lap speeds have been hovering around 229 and change, with the occasional lap in the 230s. This is very good news. This is as fast as anyone has gone all month. This is very good news, not only for Bourdais, but for his team, Dale Coyne Racing and, coincidentally enough, for me.

F Bombs

Dale Coyne is a friend of Bill Healey (more about him later) and the person responsible for me getting into this year's 500. Technically speaking, I am an employee of Dale Coyne Racing, so although I am supposed to be an unbiased journalist it's pretty easy for me to be rather biased in this instance and root for Bourdais.

I am glued to the screen, leaning forward, sitting on the edge of the couch. He heads off onto lap 3. Into and through turn one he is not slowing down at all; his corner entry speeds are flickering at 237 mph. He swings on through the short chute heading into turn two. My eyes see it before my mind fully registers it: twitch? slide? A little bit of a slide at the back end?

As my mind is processing that, just past the apex of two and around 230 mph, the back end steps out a lot. A foot, maybe 18 inches. Bourdais countersteers into it and the front end grabs, sending him straight in the direction his front wheels were pointing: Straight at the outside wall at a speed of 228 mph. The moment of impact coincides with the next words out of my mouth:

"FUCK!!!"

I scream loud enough to literally rattle the Mountain Dew can sitting on the end table. The impact is massive and vicious.

Vicious Impacts

He hits the wall at a slightly oblique angle, later calculated to be about 20 degrees from head on. This will be the first of many small blessings that will start to add up. The entire right side of the car, from the front wing back through the wheels and suspension, and including the right-hand side pod, explodes. Carbon fiber, aluminum, magnesium alloy, steel: are all rendered into what appears to be a fine powder. The car caroms off the wall and slides down into the middle of the track, then tumbles into a slow, sickening half roll. It slides on its right side for what seems like a week and a day, then flops back upright and comes to a stop.

From where the car comes to rest, all the way back to the point of impact, the track is littered with bits and pieces no bigger than a candy wrapper. It looks like a plane crash. The words "debris field" form in my mind as a handful of safety vehicles arrive on the scene.

The camera zooms in a bit, and you can see Bourdais sitting in the cockpit, head moving slightly. I wait. You have to wait. This is, sadly, not the first time I've seen something like this. Movement from the driver is good, but it can also be deceiving. The driver could be alive, or he could be quickly on the way to being dead, with his body just twitching through its final autonomic functions. Bourdais moves again. This time his hands come up and try to open the visor on his helmet, a sign to the safety crews that he is all right. I inhale for the first time. He can't get the visor open. His movements are slow and logy. "Blood loss," I start to worry. "Concussion," I add to the list.

Tension Building

Although the cars are designed to not do this, here is the slight chance that a big metal piece – an A-arm or something along those lines – penetrated the cockpit and then stabbed into Sebastien. He could be bleeding out. The safety crews are everywhere at once. The first responder is kneeling where the right-side pod used to be only seconds before. He is leaning in, talking intently to Bourdais through his helmet.

The emergency crew doctor arrives seconds later, leans in from the left-hand side, and exchanges a few terse words with the other safety guy and Bourdais. The doctor nods once, gets up from his knees and straddles the car at the scuttle, right in front of the windscreen, and leans forward into Bourdais face.

"Oh shit..." I murmur.

He's not dying, but this is not good. Not good at all.

They are not extracting him from the car. They are urgent, but it looks like he's not going to be getting out of the car any time soon. That is a bad sign. His injuries can't be determined from this distance and while he is shrouded within the car's safety cell. The camera zooms back out to wide. Now there are a dozen; two dozen; lots of safety crew members all over the place. Spreading out oil dry. Brooms everywhere. It looks like they are trying to sweep up an area the size of two football fields that are raggedly covered with tortilla chips. An ambulance pulls up as the crew, under the direction of the on-scene doctor, begins the extraction process. It is somewhat reminiscent of a bomb demolition crew from a movie; everyone is moving slowly and deliberately. Gently, gently. No sudden movements. Don't jerk anything.

Talking Heads

I become aware of the broadcast crew yammering and gibbering. They are, like most racing announcers, horrid. They have that need, perhaps directed from the producers, to fill the space. Keep talking. No dead air.

We go to commercial.

When we come back, Sebastien Bourdais is out of the car and on his way, by ambulance, to IU Health University Hospital (or Methodist Hospital, as old timers like me still call it). This is semi-good news, or at least the news is steadily improving. The trauma center at Methodist Hospital has the best orthopedic emergency center on the planet. Period. No one even comes close. If you think about it for a while, you can realize why. Bourdais is now headed this way, and if anyone can keep him alive and in one piece after an impact like that, it will be the orthopedic emergency center at Methodist Hospital.

The ABC broadcast crew, a Three Stooges-level group of lackwits comprised of Allen Bestwick, Eddie Cheever, and Scott Goodyear (an ignorant commentator, a quarter-talented driver from years past, and a nearly-no-talent driver from the same era) are still jabbering, still filling space, irritating me more and more with each passing word.

"Say it," I beg. "Say the words I want to hear."

A few seconds later, Bestwick says, "Medical is saying that Sebastien Bourdais is stable and has arrived at University of Indiana Hospital. He is awake and alert and never lost consciousness during the accident."

"Awake and alert.? Thank God!" I cry.

Not So Happy Gilmore

Short of a driver either dying outright or dying quickly after the accident, unconsciousness is the next biggest fear in this business. When a driver is unconscious, it can mean an entire raft of potentially bad things, starting with a concussion and going all the way up to brain death. Sebastien Bourdais is none of these things. Not even close. He's not in great shape, but it looks like he isn't going to die either. In the hours to come it will turn out that, as bad as this hit was, it could have been a lot worse.

Bourdais hit the wall at an oblique angle of 20 degrees off center. If he had hit it head-on, the G loading would have been catastrophically higher, and the bones in his lower legs, from his toes to his patella, would have been effectively rendered into paste. The safety measures in the car did their jobs exactly as they should under the circumstances. The safety cell remained intact, keeping the driver in one solid cocoon. Although it was a single, solid hit, the energy absorbing structures did their jobs, lessening the impact. A little.

Telemetry data would later show that impact registered 100 Gs. Telemetry data would also later show that Bourdais was doing 220 mph at the time of impact. IU Health University Hospital would issue an official statement saying Sebastien Bourdais had sustained a broken right hip and had broken his pelvis in seven places. Physics tried to snap him in half sideways at the waist.

Welcome to The Greatest Spectacle in Racing. This isn't golf.

Chapter 2: St. Elmo's Fire

I was fully intending to write a story on a completely different subject, but St. Elmo got in the way. I am, in all honesty, slightly tipsy as I write this. St. Elmo is a place that encourages such things. Besides, as Ernest Hemingway famously said, "Write drunk, edit sober."

In 1902, a restaurant and bar called St. Elmo opened in downtown Indianapolis. It's one of those places with overdone booths, lots of paneling, and a mosaic tile floor in front of the enormous bar.

The place must have been a speakeasy during Prohibition. It's right out of central casting in that respect, and so is the entire staff. Over-dressed in stiff formal shirts, they all seem comfortable and unflappable. Our waiter, Brett, is a comic book good-looking fellow – graying at the temples, 1,000-watt smile, consistently personable – and a fantastic waiter.

Wall of Fame

Why, you might ask, am I wasting space in this book and your precious time talking about a restaurant? Because since time immemorial, St. Elmo has been the place to eat if you are a driver, team owner, or a rich mechanic. The walls (which should be outfitted with mirrors so the hoi polloi of Indianapolis can watch themselves eat) are lined with pictures of famous drivers and of the track from days gone by.

"There's Mario," I think to myself, noticing a four-by-four-foot formal portrait. Autographed, of course. There are other photographs: Foyt, Unser, Unser (again), Unser (little Al), Vukovich, and more black and white shots of the starting field than I can count. I see a few of the newer drivers' shots here and there. Former Indy 500 racer Lyn St. James comes strolling in. Unnoticed by the gathering crowd, she draws my attention like a magnet. Shorter than I expected, she's still frighteningly cute and charismatic and capable of driving a car 50% faster than I will ever be able to; everything a boy like me would like.

Bill Healey and I are sitting at our table in the bar section, chatting with Brett before he puts in our order.

Bill, with the casual ease of one local to another, asks, "Anyone been in?"

"Anyone," in this case, means drivers or recognizable team personnel.

"Oh sure," Brett replies. "Mario was in just a little while ago," he continues, looking around as if he's wondering where one of the most prominent people in the history of auto racing had wandered off to. When I mention Bill is an old friend of Mario's (Andretti bought Bill's grandparent's home in '65 when he moved to Speedway from Nazareth, Pennsylvania), Brett goes all agog. They trade stories for a few before Brett goes and places our order.

The Signature "Elmo Cola" is a local favorite. A glass-bottled Coke or Diet Coke is mixed with the St. Elmo exclusive "Infusion," made with Maker's Mark Bourbon, imported Italian Luxardo Maraschino Cherries, and Madagascar Vanilla Beans. It's served with the restaurant's famous Drunken Cherries. The Infusion can be ordered straight up, on the rocks, as a Manhattan, or an Old Fashioned.

Soon he returns with Elmo's signature dish: Shrimp cocktail.

Savory Sensations

Yes, St. Elmo is a steak place – a very, very good steak place as it turns out – but they are, for some unexplained reason, known far and wide for their shrimp cocktail. I am not a big fan of shrimp in general, or shrimp cocktail for that matter, but hey, this is what the restaurant in Indy that all the drivers go to is known for, so of course I'm going to try it.

"This is Kosher, right?" I ask Brett as he approaches with a chilled silver bowl.

"Kosher as can be!" he says without missing a beat, adding a face-imploding wink that is all dimple and smiles. As he sets down the bowl of four shrimp drowning in cocktail sauce, I notice he is not wearing a wedding ring. A given percentage of the women in Indy have probably dated this guy, I think to myself, with an inward sigh known only to those of us who are not cartoonishly handsome.

"Gentleman, you have been warned," Brett said before turning smartly and moving away.

Moment of Truth

He is, of course, referring to the cocktail sauce itself. It is famously high-octane stuff. I can see chunks of horseradish floating within. I spear a shrimp, set it on the small side plate, and chop off a chunk with the absurdly tiny shrimp cocktail fork provided. "Wow," I think to myself, "pretty good." I immediately segment off another chunk.

Before I have completely swallowed it, my eyes tear slightly, and I feel my pupils snap closed to the size of pinheads. My sinuses feel like a domed NFL stadium with the doors open; light, airy, with a slight breeze entering from the south/southwest. Briefly I can see through time. It's like shrimp flavored with napalm and sugar. Without hesitation, I eat the rest of shrimp #1 and move directly onto #2. It goes without saying the steak was fantastic. Shoot, the baked potato was fantastic. And don't get me started on the bread.

Brett comes and goes from time to time. We chat: Where are we sitting at the track for the race? How many races has Healey gone to? All of them, his entire life, since he was a baby. Where am I from? The middle of the desert.

"Come back anytime," Brett says, and he either means it or is so good at his job he can lie with complete conviction.

Quintessential Indy

I pick up the check. I owe Healey. He's bought me so many dinners over time, that alone should be enough. But Bill is also responsible for lining things up and getting me into the 500 itself. Bill knows people. When your grandparents sell their house on 16th to a young Italian racer in 1965, you know people. When your uncle has a place two houses down, also on 16th, and was a track guard during World War II, you know people. When you're lifelong friends with Clint Brawner, you know people. When A.J. Watson calls you out in a crowd at the supermarket, and comes up to shake your hand, you know people. When you are sitting and writing in a house that is within 2 blocks of 16th and Georgetown Road, you know people.

You also know that when you come to the races, and someone asks, "Where should we go for dinner?" St. Elmo is, and will always be, the answer.

Inside the 1933 Lounge at St Elmo Steakhouse, 127 S. Illinois St., Indianapolis, Indiana.

Chapter 3: The Quiet Racer

It's Thursday. The day is cold and overcast, threatening rain. The immense track is largely quiet, just spots of activity here and there. We wander through Gasoline Alley; all the garages are quietly busy with preparations for something that will be happening soon enough. For the first time in a long time, I get a smell of ethanol. The odor of sickly sweet, decaying flowers makes me inhale deeper.

Apart from Pippa Mann, all long blond hair and a bright smile that seems to be saying, "I'm quicker than most of the boys here," none of the drivers are around.

Until I get to the last garages, and there's Ed Carpenter.

Hometown Hero

You can tell what Ed Carpenter looked like when he was, say, 12: just like he looks now, only shorter. He's one of those guys that always looks like a kid. If he didn't have a day's growth of beard, you'd think he was a college sophomore. Healey knows him, so we walk right in. I get introduced, and we shake hands. His hands are warm and papery and he clamps down like a flesh-covered vice. It's a hazard of the profession. All race car drivers have a grip strength somewhere right around the bite force of a crocodile.

Carpenter is one of these odd throwbacks to what drivers were like 50 or 60 years ago. He is a local kid, born and raised in Speedway. His presence has the effect of a Mercury astronaut: He's quiet, personable, and gives you the feeling you wouldn't have to scratch that deep to find a bottomless well of self-confidence when he gets behind the wheel of a car. His smile is huge and genuine, and sort of reminds me of Mark Donohue; he's like a sincere schoolboy who excels at getting away with practical jokes. Carpenter is the nephew of the Georges (a branch of the track-owning Hullman family) so yeah, that did open more than a few doors for him. But that will only get you so far in the racing business. Sooner or later you will have to produce, and Ed Carpenter did.

By his own admission, he's not very competitive on road courses, so he's turned into a high-speed oval specialist. Indeed, during qualifying, he was the fastest Chevy powered car out there, qualifying 2nd overall.

Fine & Dandy

"How's the car?" Healey asks. The implication is that he is surrounded by Hondas, and the next Chevy is his teammate J.R. Hildebrand four spots back; then even more Hondas and finally the first of the mighty Penske-Chevrolet runners, Will Power in ninth.

"Oh good. We're fine," he says, and that's what stops me hard. It's the way he said, "We're fine," that I notice. It was a simple and declarative statement, sort of like the response to his favorite color. I have noticed, over the years, there is one kind of driver to watch out for at the Indy 500. Usually, amidst all the hubbub and noise, among all the racers that are going fast and being interviewed on TV, there will always be a few racers (usually just one) up there at the front of the pack: Head down, quietly going about their business, clocking lap after lap after lap, and doing it quickly.

And with that simple "We're fine," I realized Ed Carpenter is that racer.

Potential Happenings

I watch him and Healey chatting away as I think to myself, "Shoot, this guy's gonna win the whole thing, isn't he?" There are no sure things in racing. Never. And although I would not bet, or say unequivocally that Ed Carpenter is going to win this thing, he is suddenly very much in my consciousness. Carpenter could win the Indy 500. He could do it, and it wouldn't surprise me at all.

Chapter 4: Hang Ten

To me, there are three high holy days on the racing calendar. The first is the Italian Grand Prix. Much like Eskimos having many words for snow, the Italians have their own singular word for *racing fans*: Tifosi. And Monza, home of the Italian Grand Prix, is the cathedral where we Tifosi worship.

The greatest drivers in the world have raced here, and every year the Grand Prix is a fine Italian opera played out at over 200 miles an hour.

The 24 Hours of Le Mans is next. Held close to the summer solstice each year, it started out as a twice around the clock endurance grind, but now is more like a sprint race for maniacs. This is where sports car racing was perfected. This is where, up until the late 60s, street legal two-seaters from Jaguar and Ferrari and Ford and Porsche slugged it out to see who was best over public roads, come rain or shine, day or night, every year.

The last high holy day is the Indy 500. The race is held at Indianapolis Motor Speedway located in the small Midwestern town of Speedway, Indiana. It seems rather simple at first. The track resembles an enormous cafeteria tray, essentially a rounded rectangle. It is very wide, very smooth, and slightly banked. There are only four turns and all of them are left handers, how hard can it be? As it turns out, it is very hard largely due to one thing: Speed.

Hurricane Force

A modern Formula 1 car, trimmed out and on a high-speed track like Spa or Monza, can hit a top speed of 215 or so. A modern sports prototype at Le Mans can do about the same. A modern Indy car averages over 225 during the race. Averages. The corner entry speeds this year were flickering into the high 230s. The best analogy I have for high speed oval racing – a thing, bizarrely enough, invented by the Italians (okay, Romans) and made famous in the movie Ben Hur – is, curiously, big wave surfing.

Think of surfing, and most people see a place like Banzai Pipeline or Oahu's North Shore. Pipeline is very reminiscent of the Grand Prix. Technical and fast, with waves in the 20-foot range, breaking directly over a bed of razor sharp coral. Getting it wrong means getting munched in a very spectacular and public way. Racing at Indy is like Waimea Bay. The waves are huge and powerful. They are easily over 30 feet high; as any surfer will tell you, the bigger the wave is, the faster it travels. If you even catch the wave at Waimea, which means enduring a fear-inducing 20-foot elevator drop, you then have to make the bottom turn, a simple graceful arc to your right, or you get eaten alive by literally tons of ocean that cleans you off your board and, if you're lucky, drives you straight down into the bottom and rolls and tumbles and smashes you for, potentially, the last 50 yards of your life.

Brian Kalama, full-blooded Hawaiian, son of the great Buffalo Kalama, lifeguard at Makaha, and famed big wave surfer, put it this way: "The problem with big wave surfing is that when something goes wrong, it goes real wrong, real fast." And that, in a nutshell, from a completely different walk of life, in 18 words, is racing at Indianapolis Motor Speedway: The problem with racing at Indy is that when something goes wrong, it goes real wrong, real fast.

Risky Roulette

The corner entry speeds, not to mention the cornering speeds themselves, are so high, the smallest mistake – being off line by inches, say, or brushing a competitor no harder than two shopping carts bumping – can lead to appalling consequences. Sebastien Bourdais was off by no more than 18 inches, the distance between your knife and fork on the dinner table, and that was enough to send him into the outside wall like a horizontally thrown lawn dart at 230 miles per hour.

Racing at Indy is so simple, it should be easy, but the speeds are so high that making a 90-degree left turn is like rolling the dice against the Devil himself. Now add 32 other speed-crazed mutants with a competitive streak that would make a test pilot blush, very large right feet, and even larger, er, attachments, and the equation of simply keeping up, let alone winning, is magnified ten thousand-fold.

Head Case

This is all done in cars with open wheels and open cockpits whose main structural components are cloth and glue. The buffeting from the wind in traffic is enough to spin you halfway to Oz and back. The levels of grip at the limit are only slightly better than those found on roads outside Anchorage in February. And all the while your head – you know, the part where your brain is kept, the part where all that is *you* is; all thoughts, all hopes, all dreams, all memories; where your fondest desires and deepest fears live – are hanging out in a 230+ mile an hour breeze just waiting to get clocked by someone else's wheel or tire or shrapnel from a crash that never even involved you in the first place.

That is the Indy 500.

Raw & Relentless

That is just what is at stake, and it will go on for two hundred laps, turn after turn, for over three hours without respite or let up. There are no time outs. There is no halftime break. There is only the green flag, then 500 miles between you and fame and victory and a long drink of cold milk on a fine May afternoon in the middle of Indiana farmland. It is a simple stage with simple rules where all that is True and Good in us vies against all that is False and Poor. This is the Indy 500. And it is Pure, and it is Righteous. Hallelujah!

Chapter 5: Female Perspective

Dale Coyne stands in stark contrast to the wisdom of Leo Durocher. He is as nice and personable as nine out of ten Midwesterners you meet, but he rarely finishes last. He is tall and perpetually grinning, seeming tubbier on television than he is in person. He has a big round Irish face dominated by a huge smile and he frequent nods when he listens. He listens a lot, intently, to whomever is talking to him, whether it's some awestruck kid or an upset racer in his employ.

He comes across as just the sort of boss you'd want: Fair as the day is long, but tough as an anvil.

Coyne is from Minooka, Illinois, and no, that's not a joke name. It's sort of south and west of Chicago, kind of by Joliet (ancestral home of Jake Blues). Minooka is, by sheer coincidence, the home of Nick Offerman, the actor that plays Ron Swanson on Parks and Recreation. In some odd way, Dale seems as if he could be Ron Swanson's fun friend; the jovial Yin to Swanson's brooding Yang.

Steadfast Vision

Dale Coyne has been racing since the early 80s and has an air about him that makes you think he's forgotten more about racing than you will ever know. He is, to accurately use the term, a fixture in the series. Dale can do more with a nickel than Chip Ganassi can do with a Ben Franklin. And that is yet another charming facet of Dale Coyne, the racer.

He always can put a team together. He's money conscious, yes, but no more so than any other team owner. I recall him saying one of the reasons he got out of the first gen IRL, and back into CART, is that at the time, the IRL was all ovals. "There are no small wrecks on ovals," he said. "Whenever one of my guys wrecks, the entire car is totaled, gone, a complete write-off. I just can't afford to wreck that many cars."

Another thing Dale has a knack for that everyone in the series admires: He's a fantastic talent scout. He has this wonderful ability to find drivers, seemingly out of nowhere and largely unsung, who turn out to be either great talents or fantastic journeymen teammates. Dominic Dobson, Randy Lewis, Buddy Lazier, Paul Tracy, Roberto Moreno, Memo Gidley, Alex Barron, Ryan Dalziel, Cristiano da Matta, Katherine Legge, Bruno Junqueira, Justin Wilson, and Conor Daly all got their start in big time American racing with Dale Coyne. He's like Sam Phillips at Sun Records, minus Elvis Presley but plus Paul Tracy.

Female Touch

This year he's running Sebastien Bourdais (who sadly crashed out in qualifying), James Davidson (Bourdais' replacement), Ed Jones, and Pippa Mann. Davidson is some sort of crazed miracle worker, jumping into Bourdais' car with only half an hour of practice under his seat before starting the 500. Ed Jones is, like 86% of Dale's past drivers, a young up-and-comer. Pippa Mann, on the other hand, is no stranger to the speedway. She shows up every year and beats about a third of the field in qualifying with little to no practice.

This delights me to no end because it upsets the sclerotic old dinosaurs who grumble out horse manure about "women can't" and other such chauvinistic crap that should have ended decades ago. My fondest wish is to be sitting in the stands when a woman finally wins the 500, and to be sitting right next to one of these dingbats. Watching him faint will be the cherry on top.

Calm & Collected

Dale is married to, and I am not making this up, Gail Coyne. She's as sweet as he is. Short, blond, nods while listening and, even better, is responsible for Sonny's Barbeque (Dale's main sponsor for most of this season). I'm not sure if she owns it, runs it, bought or whatever, but she understands barbecue, that's for sure.

"Have you ever been to Florida?" she asks rhetorically. "Barbecue is like a religion to those people."

"Like a religion to those people," I jokingly respond, "shoot, it's like a religion to me!"

She laughs as we dive deep into the sociology of soul food generally, and barbecue specifically.

Whenever she talks, Dale listens attentively, and vice versa. Dale and Gail make make a great couple. They both radiate the same vibe: comfort and confidence. It must be a huge tension reliever to be a driver in that environment. No matter how tense things get, there's Dale, all calm and cool with a seemingly bottomless well of experience. Even the way he stands seems to say, "Don't worry, I can handle this."

Dale seems happy and content, because, in a certain way, he's already won: He's doing what he loves, and he has a great life with Gail by his side. If that's not winning I don't know what is, Leo Durocher's opinion notwithstanding.

Chapter 6: The Fearless Spaniard

He is calm and quiet, and precise in his movements both in and out of the arena. Fernando Alonso gives the impression of being unwavering and brave. He was all the rage at Indianapolis Motor Speedway this year, having chosen to forgo running at Monte Carlo in a sadly noncompetitive car, and having a tilt at the Indy 500. He's never run on an oval, let alone raced on one. Yet he managed to be at or near the top of the time sheets for every session he ran and managed to qualify fifth. He has outpaced such Indy luminaries as Juan Pablo Montoya and Marco Andretti.

The international press, led by a throng of Spanish reporters, mobbed him everywhere he went. Last year, there were two Spanish reporters at the track. This year there were 25. Alonso was gracious with the press and even thanked them in a post-race conference.

Concise & Precise

Alonso is twice a World Driving Champion. At the time of his first championship win, he became the youngest ever winner at only 24. He is quick and methodical, fearless and precise on the track. To win his first championship he took apart The Great One, Michael Schumacher, piece by piece, corner by corner, race by race: A seasoned professional at 24.

In Speedway, Indiana, he carried on in the same manner. He showed no signs of rashness or impulsiveness. He was smooth and mistake-free from the moment he rolled onto the track, and comfortable even at the immense speeds this track brings. His style was easy to see during practice: Closer, ever closer to the car in front, whether chasing a veteran or an impetuous young gun. Trail them down the main straight. On the rear wing through one. Closer still in the short chute and out-accelerating his opponent exiting two. Leaving him as if he had been doing it for years.

The Bullfighter

He is the new Belmonte. His suit of lights is fireproof and adorned with the names of corporations. His feet never waver or shake in the ring. Each corner is a faena. Each pass an estocada. He is unwavering and true. If he can remain unwavering and true he will attain new heights. No Spaniard has ever won the Indianapolis 500, and although this year wasn't his year, if there is to be a Spaniard to drink milk on this sacred track, it will be him.

Interlude: The Indy 500 is Pure and Righteous

I'm standing on the back patio at Healey's house in Speedway. It's like I've stepped out of a time machine. Speedway, Indiana is, apart from the track itself and occasional view of the skyscrapers in downtown Indianapolis, a place locked in time, frozen in amber. Most if it is, anyway, and Bill's neighborhood is especially so. 90 percent of the buildings seem to have been built either just before The Great War, or just after. And now, standing on the bricks of Bill's back patio, I can see a dozen back yards just like this.

All the houses are the same, yet slightly different. They were all, seemingly, built just pre-war. Two- or three-bedroom places with one bath. The houses pushed forwards towards the street (with sidewalks!), the detached garages pushed towards the back of the lots. Bill told me that one of the selling points from the developers was that each home came with two mature oak trees. So the whole street, and therefore the whole parcel of land, is covered in leafy shadows and swaying branches. If I hopped the fence and went a couple of streets over - everyone's yards are separated from everybody else's yard by a fence, white picket, of course - I wouldn't be at all surprised to find hearts carved into the bark of the trees, with inscriptions like "JB + NR = Love, 1937."

The whole place looks like a giant, real, *Leave It to Beaver* set. It's nostalgia in three dimensions. It is the middle of the middle of the bell curve; a little step to the left or the right, and you'd suddenly find yourself getting crazy and listening to Perry Como and thinking cigarettes might be bad for you.

All of that is a given, or as much as a given as America can muster, year in year out, in the middle of the heartland, in the middle of the middle of the bell curve. As much as America has a fixation with concepts like "normal" and "secure" and "predictable," we are, societally, a fairly dynamic country. We have no problem filling in wetlands and demolishing old buildings to put up new glass and steel high-rises.

History seems to be hard for us Americans to get our minds and our hearts wrapped around. Oh sure, we love to throw the word "history" around, but we usually do it in terms of something that happened five NBA finals ago. We also seemingly love and use the phrase 'We're a young country' often. We use it a lot when making excuses for some monumental societal screw up. As in, "How were we supposed to know that dumping so much industrial waste into the Cuyahoga River would make it catch fire? 'We're a young country!'" or, "Okay, okay. So we shouldn't have napalmed that third world country flat, poisoned their people and just left, but 'We're a young country!'" I think Europeans have been using that phrase, "You're a young country," as more or less a warning, for a long time. I think we've never cottoned onto that fact. Americans hear someone from, say, Germany intone, "Yes, you have elected him your President. But, you are a young country," and we take it as a compliment. "Hey, did ya hear that? We're young! We're on the move! We're not old, like The Old World. We're new! We're hip! We're happening, Baby!"

So, for us, for Americans, history - true history, something with lasting impact, something that has the force of many, many years behind it - can be hard to truly comprehend. We think things like the Super Bowl or the Emmy Awards have a long and rich history, but both have been around about as long the transistor.

History, actual history, something that has been around for hundreds of years, turns out to be very hard to find in this country, and not just because 'We're a young country!' It is because, by and large, we don't value history very much, despite our words to the contrary. Maybe we will, one day. Maybe, sometime in the future, sometime after we've lost something important and irrevocable we'll be able to understand why history is valuable: We learn from it.

So far, most Americans, and most American institutions, have a mindset that there is no capital-T-truth. That we can bend it and shape it and make it what we need it to be, moment to moment, day to day, year to year, decade to decade. Because of our belief that all is malleable, even Truth, history, our history, can be hard to understand. We can take it, hook, line and sinker, that something is Important because the inescapable hype machine has been telling us so via a media system that even Marshall McLuhan and Tim Berners Lee couldn't come up with after an entire sheet of blotter acid.

We can Believe that the ceremonial awarding of the Harley Earl Trophy at the Daytona 500 upon the hallowed ground of the Coca-Cola Winner's Circle™ sponsored by Pepsi-Cola™ is a Big Deal because they've told us it is. Even though that only happened for a couple of years about a decade ago, and NASCAR has since realized they cannot sell the naming rights to the ground to one company that makes sugar water and then sell the naming rights to the ceremony that happens on that same ground to a different company that makes sugar water. 'We're a young country!'

So History, when you really find it in America, can be a rare and beautiful thing.

The people that run the Indy 500 know this. This year's race marks the 101st running of the race. The Indy 500 has been around a lot longer than the National Football League. It has been around more than twice as long as NASCAR. That reason alone - the fact that the Indy 500 has been existed for almost as long as this country has been around - renders it exceptional and priceless. The Indy 500 represents more than the spectacle, more than the technological innovations, more than even the racing itself. It is a through-line in American and world culture that is nearly irreplaceable.

Go to a cafe in Italy, grab a random Italian and ask them to name a car race, and nine times out of ten they'll say, "The Indy 500." Grab a random German walking down the street in Zuffenhausen and ask them to name a car race, and nine times out of ten they'll say, "The Indy 500." Talk to someone in Tiananmen Square and ask them to name a car race, and nine times out of ten they'll say, "The Indy 500." We have, somehow, and most likely not on purpose, made something that is part of the world's culture. And how often can we say that? Jazz? Yes, that's us. Rock and Roll, yup, we invented that too, along with the electric guitar; but lasting worldwide cultural impact is something we don't do very much of in the U. S. of A.

And on this bright Spring day here, on a quiet street in Speedway, Indiana, I am aware of the contribution and lasting impact of The 500 because I'm standing on the back patio at Bill Healey's house. It's about ten feet square and made of brick. If you look, you can see that the bricks say:

INDIANA

PAVING BLOCK

BRAZIL IND.

The bricks Bill's father used to make this patio once paved The Speedway itself. I am standing on the very same racing surface that Ray Harroun won on, that Mauri Rose won on, that the mercurial and doomed Frank Lockhart won on, that Billy Vukovich won twice in a row on and died, while leading, going for three in a row on. These bricks are not uncommon around here - there were 3.2 million of them used to pave the track - but the idea of having your patio paved with them strikes me as being cool as only Americans can do it.

I am reminded of the line from *Raiders of the Lost Ark*: "We are simply passing through history. This, this is history." America has rolled on like a fleet of bulldozers, building, destroying, rebuilding, and starting anew over and over in a dizzying repetition of folly and success, foolishness and triumph. History is hard for us. Hard for us to grasp, and harder still for us to hold onto; and more's the pity, because, at the heart of it, we are a young country and we have yet to know our full worth or fully realize what we might lose. We only grasp our potential, so far.

History is hard to know, because of all the hired horse manure, but sometimes, history is right under your feet.

Chapter 7: Speedway Legends

I have a friend, Bill Healey, and in so many ways, all this is his fault. I met him over a decade ago when he was starting up a Motorsports sponsorship company and needed a writer. At that time, I was only a writer when it was needed. I worked on corporate communications and designing computer games and stuff like that. But I did know how write, and I did grow up in a car and racing family, so why not give it a try?

And that's how Bill and I became friends.

Under The Bridge

For years Bill, a native of Speedway, Indiana who has attended the 500 every year of his life, was haranguing me to come out and see the race. This year I was finally able to do it, and discovered one of my greatest sources of charm and fascination was being around the track and Speedway and Indianapolis with Bill. And yeah, sure, the racing conversation was flying fast at almost every hour of the day, but I found the constant running commentary about everything else that supported racing here in Speedway even more fascinating.

On the Thursday before the race, we were driving around the track in Bill's car. He was keeping up a running commentary, only about 10% of which I expected.

"Right here," Bill said, pointing to a nondescript portion of the back stretch. "This is where that walk-over pedestrian bridge was. That's right where Vuky (the old timers' nickname for Bill Vukovich, two-time 500 winner) died. He got thrown off the track and ran into the abutment for the bridge... that was right in front of me."

Fond Memories

"See all the turn three stands? There used to be a big grove of oak trees there. Me and my brother-in-law and so-and-so used to know the farmer that owned the land. It was great squirrel and rabbit hunting there. But then they built up the stands there and tore out all the trees. Damn race track," Bill said with a laugh.

He loves racing more than anything and would gladly give up squirrel hunting for it.

Driving around the town of Speedway was much the same. It was a constant stream of stories from high school: "I dated so-and-so who lived in that house. She was really cute, great kisser too." He said this with a certain gleam in his eye, the kind that only a 70 year-old-man with a fond memory can have. "That's where Clint Brawner lived. He used to park the race cars in his front yard before the race," or, "I saw George Bignotti filling up his car, a brand new Buick, at that old gas station."

It was that growing sense of background radiation this town has, and that Healey conveyed, which makes Speedway so enthralling. For a race fan like me, it must be like living in Cocoa Beach, Florida would be for a space exploration fan. Everywhere you look is something, big or small, that you either directly know about or that influenced stuff you heard about as a racing fan. For example, Bill and I were driving down Georgetown Road (Indianapolis Motor Speedway is located at the corner of 16th and Georgetown Roads) and he was pointing to the empty stretch of fields now bordering the track: "That was the Johnson house, and right there was Long's, and that was my grandparents' house," pointing to a spot in a field, now a parking lot every Memorial Day weekend.

"That was the house they sold to Mario?" I asked.

"Well, Clint Brawner, yeah, but he got it for Mario."

With Every Fiber

Brawner was an old school car builder/team honcho. He used to wrench for the great A.J. Watson, but then struck out on his own and ran teams at the 500. In 1965, Brawner hooked up with this new hot-shoe from Nazareth, Pennsylvania named Mario Andretti. Mario and Bill met when he was moving to his new house, and they've been friends ever since.

It feels like that's how it is here for everyone, but Bill is a little bit more emblematic than most. This is all personal. Famous racer so-and-so lives right around the corner. The kid that delivers your newspaper (people still get newspapers on their doorstep around here) also delivers it for a team owner. Your nephew is on the same basketball team with a chief mechanic's kid... it is literally never ending. The Indy 500 isn't what these people do in May every year, it's who they are.

This was no better illustrated than when Bill and I were walking through the paddock of the historic Indy car race. There were several dozen old Indy race cars all lined up, waiting to be driven around the track on show laps for the fans: Pre-war Millers and big roadsters from the 50s, on up to the modern day. As we walked the rows, taking them all in, Bill didn't mention the races they were in or who drove them. He already knew that by heart. Bill's information was much more personal:

"Oh yeah. That's Agabashian's car. I used to cut his grass when I was in 4th grade. That guy's mechanic had a kid sister that everybody in high school wanted to date. My friend John drove over his mailbox one Saturday night."

Car after car, known today as only blurry photos and statistics, Bill Healy knows, and now I do too, as catalysts for things much more personal, much more immediate, and much more lasting.

Chapter 8: Barrel Roll

Watching the Indy 500 from my perch in the top floor of the press center was interesting. At first, I was surprised at how professional all the drivers were. They dropped the green flag and they all snarled off into turn one with seemingly little drama.

It was sort of like standing by the barrel of an enormous shotgun that was fired every 40 seconds or so.

Quiet Sunday

For the longest time, the laps just clicked off. Nobody did anything stupid. There were no gonzo dives for the inside, no low percentage moves that were doomed to failure. The racing was just as clean as could be. The first round of pit stops was largely the same way. My spot was directly behind Simon Pagenaud's pit box and a little off from where Hélio Castroneves was. It was amazing to watch the Penske pit crews do their jobs with flawless precision.

The press center is a four-story building right next to The Panasonic Pagoda, the tall timing and scoring tower. The top is a glass box that can easily accommodate 125 members of the press. There are screens everywhere, and we got the direct audio feed from race control so we knew when they'd throw yellow flags, and when they'd go back to green.

About half the press stayed at their desks – long rows of tables with power and data hook ups – either banging away on laptops or staring at the TV feed on the screens. The rest of us were lined up along the windows, watching the cars, now broken up into packs of 8 or 10, blasting down the straight, over the yard of bricks, and into turn 1 doing 230 or so. Then as the cars zoomed out of sight, we would all turn to the screens and watch until they came back around again.

Airborne Assault

This was our rhythm until, on lap 53, backmarker Jay Howard either drifted up into the gray exiting turn 1, or was pushed up there by Ryan Hunter Reay (it depends on who you ask). He slithered up into the outside wall, then slowly slid back down the track directly into the path of oncoming traffic. The main pack had already blown by us, so everyone in the media center was watching the screens when a minor screw up turned into a very bad day.

Howard's car, now damaged beyond control in the initial impact, slid back down the track and nearly missed Tony Kanaan's #10 Honda powered entry. This caused a collective exhalation from the assembled press. But now Howard's car was pretty much in the middle of the track, grinding to a halt directly in front of the oncoming Scott Dixon, who was powerless to do anything but ram Howard at around 225 mph.

Everyone in the press room let out a "ohhhh-ahhhhAAAAAHHHHH-OH!" as Dixon impacted Howard's car and was flat out launched like a low angle mortar round. Dixon, a highly personable and perennially grinning Kiwi, arced through the air, reaching an apogee of around 25 or 30 feet. Helio Castroneves appeared on the scene doing well over 200 miles an hour, and dove for the last open space, which was directly under Dixon's car, mid-parabola.

Tumble and Fall

Dixon's car was in a corkscrewing tumble by the time he was on his way down, starting to do a neat full barrel roll as Helio scooted under. His downward arc was a perfect illustration of geometry and physics until all hell broke loose. Dixon clipped the inside catch fence, started to tumble, and came down half-sideways/half-upside down onto the inside wall, directly onto his open cockpit.

This caused the assembled press to descend into inchoate screaming as Dixon's car literally ripped itself in half. The press room seemed to explode with monosyllabic gibberish. We were all educated racing journalists. We all knew, usually first hand, what the cost of this sport could be.

Now it was very hard to know where to look. Shrapnel flew everywhere. The entire rear end of the car – the transaxle, rear suspension, brakes, uprights, wheels, and tires – all sheared completely off and slung back towards the outside wall in a terrifying kinetic twist, narrowly missing the oncoming cars. Dixon's car continued its high-speed tumble, each bit of rotation shedding more and more pieces. Finally, the car came to rest, sitting upright, rendered down to the tub with the left front suspension and wheel still attached. The engine, which everyone at first thought had been sheared off, had actually been compressed forward by one of the multiple impacts, tamping it fully into the fuel tank, which miraculously remained intact and did not rupture.

As the car came to rest, the safety crews were already rolling up and, astonishingly, Scott Dixon unbuckled his belts and climbed from the cockpit.

What can only be described as a roaring silence filled the press room. Had the car rotated another 10 degrees at most, it would have struck the top of the retaining wall flat on, and no doubt torn Dixon apart, decapitated him, or both.

Miracle in Indy

Our stunned silence gave way to the wild urgent questions; everyone was asking everyone else, "What did you see? What did it look like?" As the multiple replays rolled on, everyone continued to gasp and shake their heads and mutter to themselves and one another. The replays showed that not only had Dixon really clobbered the inside wall, but his car had grabbed the debris fence like a giant hand, sweeping it aside like a curtain.

Dixon was checked and, somehow, released just minutes after the accident. He didn't have any significant injuries. Miraculous doesn't even begin to describe this outcome. Every time I see the replay it seems like there are a dozen times Scott Dixon should have died. I looked at an older, grizzled sportswriter standing next to me and asked, "what's the Powerball lottery up to?"

"What!?" was his incredulous response.

"If I was Dixon, I'd buy a lotto ticket on the way home tonight," I answered.

Chapter 9: A Wide Face

Years ago, David Bowie starred in a movie called **Merry Christmas, Mr. Lawrence**. In addition to starring Bowie, Tom Conti, and a bunch of other people, the main antagonist was played by Ryuichi Sakamoto. In the reviews, Ryuichi Sakamoto was referred to as "Japan's David Bowie," because, like Bowie, he was a musician and composer who was just getting into acting. One of the people interviewed about the movie, a Japanese film journalist, described Sakamoto as "having a wide face."

It would seem this is a Japanese term meaning, roughly, that the person is very famous.

As I looked down from my perch in the press building at Takuma Sato in the winner's circle, all huge smiles and waving, my first thought was, "Takuma Sato now has a very wide face."

Neck-and-Neck

It was a very enjoyable, thrilling, and fascinating race. Sato, or Taku or Taku-san as his fellow racers call him, became the first Japanese driver to ever win the Indianapolis 500. He did it with style, grace, and astonishing amounts of speed. It some ways, this was rather surprising. Sato has been a fixture on the IndyCar circuit for a while now, and before that, on the Grand Prix circuit. He had only won a single IndyCar event. He is, and how can I put this diplomatically, a bit of a nutcase. Sato is known for being brave and quick and seemingly fearless. He is also known for taking chances and trying gonzo passing maneuvers that rarely work, usually taking out one or more competitors in the process.

Towards the end of this year's 500, he was at the front of the field. And in the final laps, it boiled down to a two-man race between Sato and Helio Castroneves – three-time Indy champion and former **Dancing With the Stars** winner. Castroneves, a Brazilian, is outgoing, effusive, and animated to an extreme. Most Brazilians have that rep, but Castroneves is like that on top of your usual Brazilian ebullience. He is also a racer. Always fast and competitive, Castroneves races with a flair and style on top of his outright speed that makes him highly entertaining to watch. When he wins, he is known for climbing out of his car and scaling the nearest catch-fence, pumping his fists, and screaming for joy at the fans.

Hot Laps, Hot Mic

With just a handful of laps to go, it was either going to be Taku-san or Castroneves. Either way it would make history. If Sato could do it, he would be the first Japanese winner...the first Asian, period. If Castroneves won, he would join an elite group of racers who have won the Indy 500 four times. In 100 Indy 500s, only three men have won four times: A.J. Foyt, Al Unser Sr., and Rick Mears. So no matter what happened, this would be historic.

Or, Sato would go all gonzo again and crash and take them both out. Or Castroneves would let passion drive his right foot and crash and take them both out. Neither of those happened, thankfully. Castroneves tried a couple of moves on Sato going into one, but none of them worked. And down the straights, Sato's Honda-powered Andretti Racing entry had more speed than Castroneves' Chevy.

As he took the checkers, Sato, wanting to share his joy and thank the team, keyed the radio button on his steering wheel. Unfortunately, it was not the "closed channel" button to just Michael Andretti and the rest of the team. It was the "open broadcast" button and it was sent out to the entire world.

Sato was screaming like a kid at Christmas who just got every toy in the catalog. Although he is rather outgoing and known for having a huge grin continually plastered on his face, this was Sato in a full joyous explosion of sentiment. At the awards banquet later that night, Tony Kanaan, a former teammate of Sato's, and a Brazilian only slightly less outgoing than Castroneves, announced he had already downloaded Taku-san's on-air celebrations as the Sato-specific ringtone on his phone.

Nice Guys Finish First

The rare thing about Sato is how all the other drivers seem to genuinely like the guy. Everybody, even Castroneves – who desperately wanted win number four – seemed just as happy as Taku-san was. I heard from journalists, team owners, mechanics, and fellow racers that "It couldn't have happened to a nicer guy." And they were all sincere. And they were all right. Takuma Sato is just one of those nice people you run into a few times each day, only he happens to be a racer, and now a winner of the Indy 500.

Given the Japanese society's predilection for popularity, fads, and expansive love of fame, everyone said Japan was going bonkers within moments of the news. And Taku-san pretty much lost it on the podium. The traditional drink of milk from an old-time glass bottle was four huge swallows, followed by dumping the remaining contents directly onto his head while grinning and laughing. It was the image of the race. It perfectly captured how Takuma Sato felt. At that moment, I had a mental image of his face on billboards in Tokyo and Nagoya and such. Huge grin. Unbridled delight.

"Taku-san now has a very wide face," I thought.

Chapter 10: Among The Fans

Journalists are, as a group, jaded and jaundiced about the world around them. Whatever their specialty, whatever little slice of the world they cover, it's usually done so with barely concealed condescension and detachment. This is something you are more or less taught in college newswriting classes. Maintaining a sense of detachment is how a journalist stays objective.

American journalists have this fetish about being objective. But this fetishized objectiveness is the beginning of being jaded in progressively darker shades of green; jaundiced in ever-yellowing hues.

By the Book

Sportswriters, although they can (and are encouraged to) be fans of the sports they cover, are particularly focused on being objective. Just the facts, Ma'am. Hits. Runs. Strikes. Passes. Touchdowns. Scores. Statistics. Always tons and tons and tons of statistics. Especially for American sportswriters.

So there we all were, some 150 or so journalists in various shades of jaded experience, about two-thirds of the way through the 2017 Indy 500. Assiduously watching, taking notes, scribbling passages, hammering on keys. We were covering the event. Get it all down, stitch it together, write a lead-in graph or two, a nice summation and, bada-boom, bada-bing, you've met your deadline, kept your Managing Editor happy, and lived to write another day.

Sixpence Suspense

A few times during the race this professional detachment fell away, most notably during Dixon's colossal accident, but most of the time the press area was quiet mumbles and typing, with the occasional four-sentence conversation. It was in this setting, on a late race restart, that all professionalism fell away from everyone of us in that room in an instant. A pack of cars, indeed the second pack of cars behind the lead group, were all blasting down the back straight on the first green flag lap after a protracted caution period. Suddenly, for reasons that were never clear, this pack of cars, the entire pack, all saw a passing opportunity. Someone checked up, or slowed or something, and the pack – and I mean the entire pack – fanned out two – no, three – no, four – no, SIX-wide.

Everyone, and I mean literally every one of us in the top level of the pressroom, switched in that instant from being jaded, jaundiced reporters, and reverted back to what got us into this business in the first place: Race fans. Collectively, we had been around racing long enough to know what was up, what was down, and what happens when things go sideways. And what we were now looking at was directly on the edge of going very, very sideways.

From the outside wall to the infield grass, six cars were now running side by side at 230 miles an hour. The biggest gap between any two cars was maybe the width of your palm. The slightest was the thickness of your hand. As the cars fanned out, we, the assembled press, all started screaming, and I mean screaming,the exact same thing: "NO! No, no, NO, no, no, no, nononoNONONOOOOO!!!!"

Instant Fans

We knew what we were going to see next. This was bad. This was toddler-wandering-into-a-running-machine-shop bad bad. This was bad to the point of taking us out of journalism entirely. There were too many cars, too much speed, and a quickly diminishing amount of space... and then, cooler heads prevailed. It was as if all six drivers realized what they were doing and, in a snap, sorted it out.

Marco backed out of the throttle. Another car dropped left and back. Alonso (you knew Alonso was going to be in the middle of this) somehow found more speed, gained a car length, and moved right. It was over in a second, maybe a second and a half, maybe two. But in that brief span of time, we journalists were reduced to being just fans at the track, watching the race, having a blast.

Chapter 11: After The Storm

It's mid-morning in Speedway, Indiana and I walk outside into the bright Memorial Day sunshine. It is as perfect and sunny as a small-town Midwest spring day can get. Leafy green trees line the block. White clapboard houses. White picket fences. Carefully maintained yards and house-proud dwellings line the block, stretching as far as one can see. Birds tweeting and chirping. All that's missing is a towheaded paperboy with a crewcut.

This is postcard middle America to a T. Pleasantville in 3D Technicolor.

Nothing here makes it remarkable in the least, but if I were to walk ten yards to my left, there it would be: A half-mile to the east is Indianapolis Motor Speedway. A low, glowering éminence grise whose presence can be felt, night and day. It radiates through your consciousness, like a power source just into the infrared. But here, right now, there is nothing but a quiet holiday morning. Yesterday, and I mean less than 24 hours ago, the scene was utterly different.

Cordiality and Chow

Yesterday the streets, even these residential streets nominally on the periphery of The Scene, were swarmed with people. Walking ten yards to my left, which is north, would have given a better picture: A mass of humanity all moving toward the Speedway, 98 percent of them dragging coolers, hauling backpacks, carrying this and that. And all of them, all 100 percent, were jabbering and gibbering and talking and screaming and chatting and debating and conferring. And the closer you got to the track, the more intense it was. The place was awash in soda and beer and hotdogs and corndogs and deep-fried turkey legs the size of a Cro-Magnon's club.

Burgers, fries, nachos, greasy pizza slices the size of a snow shovel blade, chow mein(?!), more burgers, more corndogs; food enough to feed an army. And everywhere you looked, the mass of humanity was dressed in shorts and t-shirts and tank tops, blaring nationalist slogans or team allegiances or declarations of wanton consumption of drink and substances. And everyone was talking and burping and babbling and farting and guffawing and snorting and prattling and sweet Buddha there's a lot of them.

Normally the attendance of the Indy 500 is around three to five hundred thousand. That is roughly the number of kids that showed up at friggin' Woodstock, and this happens every year, year in, year out. And these people, these bright, perennially cheerful, down home Midwest salt of the Earth folk welcome them in. It is a stunning display of hospitality right out of some Old Testament parable. "Need to park your car? Why, here's a spot on our lawn. That'll be $20.00." The streets are lined with cars; the yards are packed with them, too. The front yards and delightful screened-in porches are full of people talking and eating and drinking. And the roads, the roads are always packed with a moving mass of humanity, going onward, ever onward toward The Track.

Picturesque Arrays

But that was yesterday. Short hours ago. Not even a full day. And now, not a speck of lawn is taken up by a vehicle. There is no trash to be seen anywhere, and I mean that: No trash. Later Healey and I do a bit of a driving tour, and the scene can only be described as stunning – but only in the context of what it was like the day before.

There was a huge parking lot the size of a shopping mall. Now it is a green, grassy field. Scores of Port-a-Potties are now neatly stacked on trailers, all patiently idling in line, waiting to merge with traffic. All souvenir booths are shuttered. Food stands that yesterday held the most common and mass-produced eats imaginable are locked down and boarded up. The garbage cans, packed to overflowing yesterday, are gone, completely gone. All refuse has vanished as if on the whim of an invisible wind god.

And the track, good Lord the track itself: A scattering of people remain here and there on the outside, but there are no signs of the throng of humanity that once was. The inside is eerie in its striking lack of people and in its neatness. Here and there are maybe a total of 150 people, where there were once hundreds of thousands. Those who are here today walk and sweep and pick up the bits of leftover trash that has so far gone unaccounted for.

Tranquil Territory

And the trash! It has all been collected up, piece by piece, and stuffed into rust-colored garbage bags, and the bags, tens of thousands of them, are neatly lined up at the end of each row of seats. The aluminum white horizontal stands, against the strong rust of the vertically arranged garbage bags, look like a Christo installation piece.

The contrast between what The Speedway brings, invites– desires, even – with what the town is now, shocks in the extreme.

Yes, this is Speedway, both in name and deed, but for the most of the year it is just a simple, small Midwestern town; one that could almost drown in its own unpretentious charm. And now, not even a day after such noise and speed and riotous behavior, Speedway, Indiana is nothing but silence and slowness and subdued conduct. It is back to as it was. Again, it is Pleasantville. It is deepest, whitest American. The heart of paleness close by the banks of the Wabash.

Chapter 12: A Slight Return: An Epilogue

Chance Encounter

We wander back toward Gasoline Alley, Bill's car idling along at a slightly-better-than-walking pace. A weary, strung out security guard half-heartedly waves us through a checkpoint. The garages are all shuttered behind steel roll-up doors... except for one. By who knows what reasoning, the remnants of Dale Coyne's team are still there. They are doing a final load-out and catching up with spares for the race. We park and get out to say hello. There, to my absolute and honest wonder, is Sebastien Bourdais. He's leaning on the back of a golf cart, talking with various team members as they walk by carrying the bits and pieces that make up a modern-day racing team.

Sebastien seems none the worse for wear, despite sitting at an odd angle and orientation – no doubt because just ten days ago, he slammed into a wall in excess of 225 mph at an impact of 100 Gs, breaking his hip and fracturing his pelvis in seven places.

He's surprisingly chatty, although he seems a bit restless and agitated. When asked how he's feeling, he answers in a world-weary way, partially because this must be the 2,459th time he's answered these same questions, but also because such questions are reminders he will not be racing for quite some time; weeks, months, who knows. Although he is as gregarious as ever, he's also a bit slow to answer. He is no doubt on enough painkillers to knock even Keith Richards on his ass.

Quiet Reflection

We chat a bit more, then take off, winding our way out through the track. We leave via the north entrance, slowly tooling by the lined-up jet-driers and safety cars, and the garages and storage sheds necessary for putting on The Greatest Spectacle in Racing.

We return home, to the leafy, tree-lined street of suburban middle America and I pause and look down the street as Bill goes inside. I think of Sebastien Bourdais, a man who shouldn't even be here. A man of uncommon talent and bravery and skill. I think of concepts like "luck" and "risk" and "mortality." But mainly I think of the racers. I think of Sebastien Bourdais.

I think of Sebastien Bourdais. I think of Sebastien Bourdais. I think of my friend/acquaintance/guy I met. I think of a man who should be dead. I think of a man who, but for the grace of God, or Fate, or Luck is still alive.

I think of Sebastien Bourdais.

Acknowledgments

Well, it's over now, but it's never over, is it?

Less than a week after "The Greatest Spectacle in Racing" wrapped up, the entire rolling circus was in Detroit for a double header race on Belle Isle as if The Indy 500 never happened. But it did, and it will be the touchstone for the following year for everyone in paddock. "Next year at Indy, I'm going to . . ." will be rattling around inside helmets and headsets until the green flag falls in the month of May in Speedway, Indiana again.

While I'm here, I'd like to recognize some of the people who made this series of articles, and now e-book, possible.

First and foremost, I'd like to thank Chris Burdick and Carl Anthony, the head guy/Founder and Managing Editor at Automoblog.net respectively. Without them, this never would have been possible, or published – or nearly as much fun.

My thanks to Bill Healey, of course, goes almost without saying. By the time I finally made it to Speedway, Bill had literally been haranguing me for years to "...come out and see The 500!" I could probably spend the rest of Bill's life cruising around Speedway from one location to the next, listening to his personal stories of drivers and cars and long-ago high school adventures gone wrong, and never tire of them or Bill's company. While I'm at it, I should also thank Bill's sister and brother-in-law, Ann and Carlton Toole, and their various kids and grandkids (too numerous to accurately remember). Ann and Carlton are a matched set and are further evidence that Bill is not just a one-off. It seems like every Hoosier I met was kind and welcoming and hospitable, and they each had enough funny stories to last a lifetime.

I'd like to thank Dale Coyne for not only being the nicest guy in racing, but also for being Bill's friend and getting me credentials. While I'm at it, the same goes for the entire IMS staff. Every one of them was professional and kind, and treated me as if I were an old friend.

I'd like to thank my family, starting with my older brothers, Terry and John, for being huge racing fans, honest wheel-men, and more than capable of discussing the finer points of racing for days on end. The same goes for my mother, surprisingly. Surrounded by men of a mechanical bent, it always seemed as if she just threw in the towel long before I was born and joyously decided to join in.

But most of all I'd like to thank my dad, Joe. This is all his fault.

Born and raised on farms and in coal mines, my father already had a natural inclination toward things mechanical. His environment did nothing to slow those inclinations down. Cars, both antique and sports-oriented, were always around the house; he always had one more than there was room to store them. Racing was the sun which my family orbited around, all thanks to Dad's astral navigation. Racing magazines and books were always neatly stacked here and there. Racing coverage, no matter how bad, was always, and I mean *always*, watched on TV. Indeed, 2017 was the first time in my life that I had ever missed broadcast coverage of the Indy 500.

And I'd like to offer an extra special thanks to my 3rd grade teacher, Mrs. Wilson, who said I was "a terrible writer"; and to Professor Kitatani, who said, "Tony, you can't write at all."

Read more of Tony's motoring prose at Automoblog.net.

Made in the USA
Lexington, KY
04 November 2017